Thank you 4 investing
in my Dreams!

— Jason D. McKay

MY FAVORITE BALLOON

Author: Jowan D. McKoy

Illustrator: Bishear JOBA

Books of Color, LLC

ISBN: 978-0-578-19295-6

Library of Congress Control Number: 2017908092

Illustrated by Bishear JOBA

PRINTED IN THE UNITED STATES OF AMERICA

This Book Belongs to:

_____

A MOM AND HER BABY
WENT OUT FOR ICECREAM
THE BABY WAS SPOILED
AND LIKED NICE THINGS

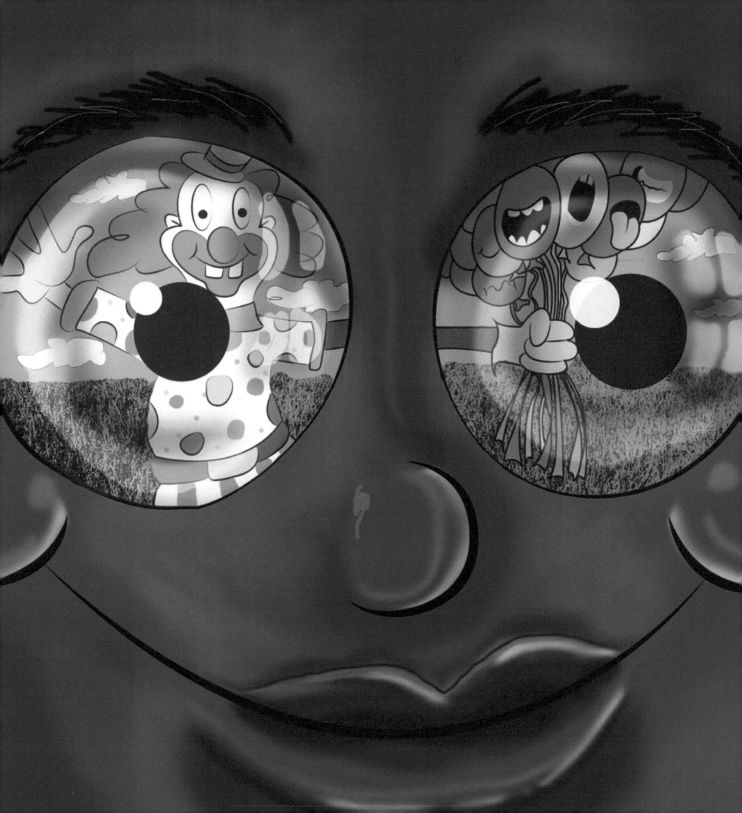

THE BABY SAW A CLOWN

SINGING A TUNE

IN ONE HAND HE HELD

A GRIP OF BALLOONS

THE MAN WAS TALL

THE BABY WAS MINI

HERE WERE SO MANY BALLOONS

THE BABY WANTED MANY

THE MOM PAID FOR TWO

BUT THE BABY GOT BLUE

E SAW WHAT THE CLOWN HAD

SO HE WANTED MORE TOO

THE MOTHER BOUGHT 5

ND WHEN THE BABY OPENED HIS EYES

HE SAW THE SURPRISE

SEVEN BALLOONS IN HIS HANDS

ALMOST ENOUGH TO LIFT HIM

OFF-LAND

TOO MANY TO HOLD

THE BABY LET GO !

THE MOTHER GRABBED ONE

WHILE THE OTHER SIX FLOAT

THE BABY WAS SAD

TO SEE THEM ALL GO

BUT WAS STILL HAPPY

O KNOW HE STILL HAD ONE

TO SHOW

THE LESSON TO LEARN
IS TO BE GRATEFUL WITH FEW
BECAUSE SOMETIMES ALOT
EQUALS LESS THAN TWO

CPSIA information can be obtained
at www.ICGtesting.com
Printed in the USA
BVHW05n1757220318
510932BV00001B/1/P